MODERN**JAZZ**
GUITARCONCEPTS

Cutting Edge Jazz Guitar Techniques With Virtuoso Jens Larsen

JENS**LARSEN**

FUNDAMENTAL**CHANGES**

Modern Jazz Guitar Concepts

Cutting Edge Jazz Guitar Techniques With Virtuoso Jens Larsen

Published by **www.fundamental-changes.com**

ISBN 978-1-78933-024-3

Copyright © 2018 Jens Larsen

Edited by Tim Pettingale

www.fundamental-changes.com

Twitter: **@guitar_joseph**

Over 10,000 fans on Facebook: **FundamentalChangesInGuitar**

Instagram: **FundamentalChanges**

For over 350 Free Guitar Lessons with Videos Check Out

www.fundamental-changes.com

Cover Image Copyright: Shutterstock, Miguel Garcia Saavedra

Contents

4

How to Use This Book

Welcome to the first of my two volumes on modern jazz guitar technique. The focus of these books is to equip you with the techniques necessary to build a modern bop-influenced jazz vocabulary for improvisation.

In this book, we will look at a number of different scales and how to apply them. In my experience, it's easy enough to look up the scale options to play over a piece of music, but much less easy to learn how to use them effectively. This book is full of solid examples that show you *how* to apply this material when playing.

Each chapter is divided into two parts: the first part discusses the musical concept; the second illustrates how to apply it to create jazz lines. I will give a brief theoretical overview and demonstrate scale exercises to practise, followed by ten licks that show different ways to apply the concept to the common II V I progression. At the end of each chapter are suggested assignments to ensure you thoroughly absorb all you've learnt.

Each chapter in this book is self-contained, but if you're new to modern jazz guitar I suggest you work through the chapters in sequence. If you are a more experienced jazz player looking for fresh ideas, you can explore any chapter and build it into your practice routine. An equally valid approach is to experiment with playing a few of the licks, then follow up by studying the underlying technique further. Jazz musicians don't seem to learn things in a linear fashion, so feel free to pick out the ideas in this book that resonate with you and let them guide what you should work on.

How to study a chapter

To add a new skill to your playing, it must be worked at until it becomes part of your musical vocabulary. This is something that students (or professionals for that matter) often get wrong when practising – not taking the time to truly "embed" new ideas. Here is how you should study each chapter:

Take Chapter Five, on the diminished scale, as an example. The first section of the chapter spells out the scale, then explains how to find the diminished scale to play over a given chord. Following on are examples of how to use the scale in a musical situation. Work through the material as follows:

1. Read and absorb the information about the scale and how to use it. This is valuable information, not to be skimmed over!

2. Play the lines and listen to the sound the scale creates over the chords. Then, to really make the scale part of your vocabulary:

3. Write your own lines using the diminished scale triads. Use the ideas to create melodies you like the sound of.

4. Work on improvising with the scale. Find some suitable backing tracks, or record your own, and jam along to them. Focus on how the scale connects one chord to another.

Composition as practice for improvisation

If you are familiar with my YouTube channel (**www.youtube.com/user/jenslarsen02**), you'll know that I often spend time composing lines and vary the material I'm using while improvising in a rubato style. This approach really helps develop the ability to compose (and therefore improvise) more musical sounding lines. It's also an effective way to explore the melodic lines you like and those you don't. Choosing to play lines that appeal to your taste is a good way to develop and define your personal style.

If you learn licks as static blocks it can be difficult to absorb them into your playing. It can also be difficult to take someone else's ideas and incorporate them into your playing in a way that sounds natural. It's not easy to find the right place for them and they can stick out – a bit like adding a line from a Shakespeare sonnet to something you've written. It's unlikely to produce a great poem!

This is why taking an idea and varying it is a helpful approach. Take my ideas and alter them in subtle ways until they sound like you. This will help you to connect the ideas with the rest of your playing.

A helpful next step is to take an idea and listen to how it sounds over a tune you're very familiar with. After that, try it over a tune you are not so familiar with. Finally, don't forget to transpose the ideas to different keys and play them in different octaves.

Get the Audio

The audio files for this book are available to download for free from **www.fundamental-changes.com.** The link is in the top right-hand corner. Simply select this book title from the drop-down menu and follow the instructions to get the audio.

We recommend that you download the files directly to your computer, not to your tablet, and extract them there before adding them to your media library. You can then put them on your tablet, iPod or burn them to CD. On the download page there is a help PDF and we also provide technical support via the contact form.

For over 350 Free Guitar Lessons with Videos Check out:

www.fundamental-changes.com

Twitter: **@guitar_joseph**

Over 10,000 fans on Facebook: **FundamentalChangesInGuitar**

Instagram: **FundamentalChanges**

Chapter One – No Alterations or Passing Notes

This chapter deals with lines that can be played using only the major scale. All examples are in the key of C Major.

If you're thinking, "This is modern jazz technique book, why are we beginning with the major scale?" there are two good reasons! First, the contemporary sounding lines we'll be playing in due course are all derived from the major scale in one way or another. Second, there is a wealth of harmonic material to be found in the basic major scale that you can use to create contemporary sounds, using substitution ideas and other concepts we will cover in due course. A lot of what you hear in jazz is created with the major scale, and not exotic or altered scales.

The Major Scale

Let's begin by looking at the construction of the basic major scale. Here is the C Major scale in a common three note per string pattern that begins in the 8th position.

Example 1a – C Major scale

When learning guitar, the focus is often on memorising scale patterns, getting the fingering right and learning to pick efficiently – rather than studying the actual notes being played. As we progress as players, however, knowing the notes is very valuable in order to play over chord changes and highlight certain chord tones. Even advanced players often don't know what notes they are playing *all* of the time, so I encourage you to learn the notes as well as memorising the scale in all its positions on the neck.

A large part of jazz is playing lines closely related to the accompanying chords. In that regard, there is no magic involved in creating great jazz, just hard work! Your time will be best spent focusing on creating interesting melodies with the tools provided in these chapters, rather than running up and down scales in an uninspired fashion. 99% of the time, the great jazz guitar solos on record use mostly simple scales and arpeggios. It is their ability to make great music from a simple idea that sets them apart.

With that in mind, let's look at the four main approaches that jazz guitarists use when they play diatonic ideas over chord changes.

Along with straight ahead scale lines, these approaches are:

• Triads

• Arpeggios

- Coltrane Patterns

- Quartal Voicings

A thorough knowledge of how chords are constructed, and how they relate to one another, opens up many possibilities for playing single note melodies. We will begin by looking at the basic triads and arpeggios as they are fundamental to everything in jazz, and address Coltrane patterns and quartal patterns as we go. Don't panic! These concepts are simply different ways to break up diatonic scales and help you to move away from playing linear melodies.

Triads

Chords and arpeggios are formed from the major scale by "stacking" intervals of a third. The most basic form of arpeggio is a triad. A triad is a strong melodic structure because it clearly spells the sound of a chord. Example 1b shows the C Major scale played in diatonic triads.

Example 1b – diatonic triads in C Major

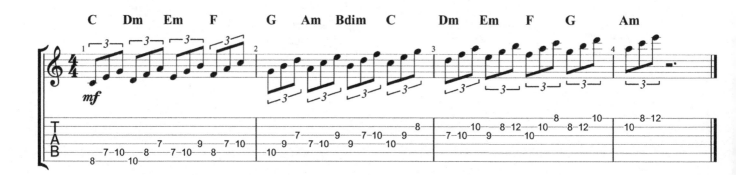

Triads are important in the sound of modern jazz because they allow us to play wider intervals which are less scale-like. Guitarists will often play triads from their root note i.e. root, third, fifth (or 1 3 5), because the root is easy to locate on guitar, but this makes for predictable sounding lines.

Playing triad ideas will generally create very strong melodies, and to create more interest, we can "re-sequence" triads. Instead of playing a 1 3 5 pattern, we can use 3 5 1, 3 1 5 or 5 1 3.

Below are the same C Major diatonic triads as Example 1b, but played with a 3 1 5 pattern.

Example 1c – diatonic triads in C Major 3 1 5 pattern

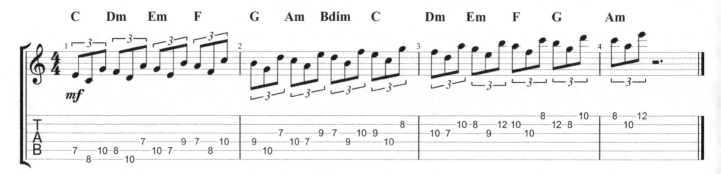

Notice that playing the triads in the above example makes them sound less like an exercise and more like a musical idea. Play through the exercise above several times to embed the sound in your ears. It's a great way to get to know your scales and to train your ears to recognise intervals.

The next example shows the diatonic triads in C Major played from the 5th instead of the root in a 5 1 3 pattern.

Example 1d – diatonic triads in C Major 5 1 3 pattern

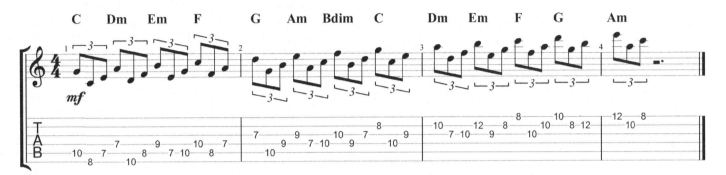

This creates a different sound again and suggests new ways of using the triads for melodic lines.

The example licks later in this chapter illustrate how triads can be used for soloing.

Diatonic 7th arpeggios

Adding the 7th note of the scale to a triad creates diatonic 7th chords (illustrated in Example 1e), which further expands the material we can use for melodic improvisation and, again, is helpful to create lines that strongly suggest the underlying chords.

Understanding how these diatonic 7th chords relate to one another creates further possibilities to increase your jazz vocabulary.

Take, for example, an Fmaj7 chord. When improvising over this chord you can use an Fmaj7 arpeggio. But you can also look for arpeggios that have notes in common with Fmaj7. The most common candidate is the one found on the 3rd (A) – Am7. Fmaj7 and Am7 have three notes in common. The Am7 arpeggio contains the same notes as Fmaj7 apart from the root, F. Mixing these arpeggios when improvising gives you more options for creating musical colours.

Example 1e walks through the diatonic 7th arpeggios in C Major. This exercise is designed to keep all the arpeggios close together in one area of the neck. Playing them this way will further embed their sound, but also help you visualise how they are connected.

Practice tip: as a brief aside, if you want to get to grips with any jazz standard, a great place to begin is to play through the whole tune using only 7th arpeggios. This will help you to hear where the harmony is going and enable you to play more melodic solos when improvising.

Example 1e – Diatonic 7th chord arpeggios in C Major:

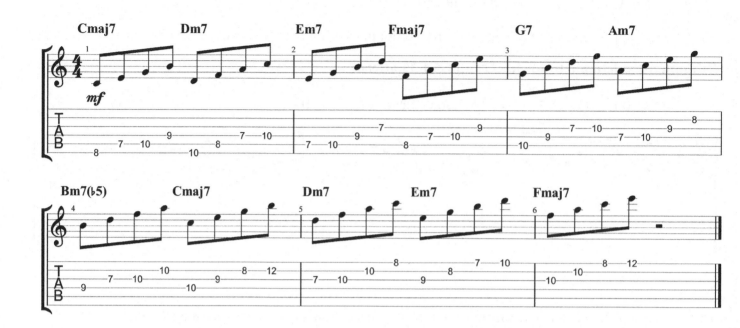

We have both diatonic triads and diatonic arpeggios available when improvising. This means that you can play much more than a G7 arpeggio over a G chord. In fact, it's a very common choice to play a Bm7b5 arpeggio over a G7 chord to create an *upper-structure* voicing.

Jazz musicians will often play a new arpeggio from any note in the underlying chord. For example, if the underlying chord is G7 (which contains the notes G, B, D and F) we will play arpeggios from the third (B) fifth (D) or even the seventh (F).

Look at Example 1e again. Find the G7 chord. Look at the arpeggios that are formed on the arpeggio notes of G7:

- Bm7b5

- Dm7

- FMaj7

This shows us that we can play a Bm7b5 arpeggio on the third (B), a Dm7 on the fifth (D) and an FMaj7 on the b7 (F).

Using arpeggios from the higher chord tones of G7, like the 5th and the 7th, means that we miss out fundamental notes like the 3rd, and therefore move away from slightly from the sound of the chord. But at the same time, by using these arpeggios we add more colorful extensions.

The following table shows you how these substitutions influence the melody notes.

Upper-structure arpeggios to play over G7

	1	3	5	7	9	11	13
G7	G	B	D	F			
Bm7(b5)		B	D	F	A		
Dm7			D	F	A	C	
FMaj7				F	A	C	E

As you can see, playing a m7b5 chord on the 3rd of a dominant 7 chord causes us to avoid playing the root (G) and adds the rich-sounding 9th (A). Playing an arpeggio on the 3rd of the chord is one of the most common uses of arpeggios in jazz. It sounds so good that many musicians always use it instead of the original arpeggio.

As you move up the chord and play arpeggios from the higher notes (5th and 7th), you include fewer notes from the original chord, so you need to be a bit more careful.

Later, we will examine the arpeggios we can use on minor 7th and major 7th chords

Diatonic Licks

Based on the concepts discussed above, let's play some lines over the II V I progression. All these lines are drawn from the C Major scale, with no alterations or added passing notes. We must work a bit harder to sound jazzy without such devices, but it is possible! Throughout, we are playing notes from the C Major scale over every chord, however we will always have an awareness of the harmony and choose notes that work well.

Example 1f uses an Fmaj7 arpeggio over the Dm7 chord (a substitution on the 3rd of the arpeggio). A Bm7b5 arpeggio is played on the G7 chord. This illustrates the technique described above, where a diatonic arpeggio is played from the 3rd of the underlying chord, and is employed by many modern jazz guitarists, such as Jonathan Kreisberg.

This lick also illustrates a common concept where a melody is created with an ascending arpeggio and a descending scale run.

Example 1f

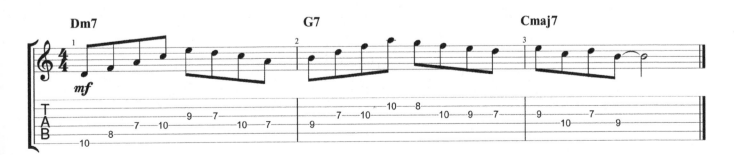

In the next example, the melodic line is constructed to seamlessly link together the arpeggios. The end of the first arpeggio encircles the beginning of the next to create a smooth transition.

Am7 and Fmaj7 arpeggio substitutions (diatonic arpeggios from the 5th and 3rd of the chord) are played over the Dm7 chord in the style of Kurt Rosenwinkel.

The line played over the G7 is a combination of two stock phrases and warrants a fuller explanation:

The first part of this phrase uses a technique known as the *Coltrane pattern*. Coltrane mastered the approach of using four-note groupings to spell out chords as a way of navigating bars that contain two chords, played at a fast tempo. He used a 1 2 3 5 pattern (the 1st, 2nd, 3rd and 5th degrees of the scale) and varied the order of the sequence to create different melodies. Here I'm playing it in reverse over the G7 chord: 5 (D), 3 (B), 2 (A) and 1 (G). Coltrane patterns are a useful way to break up scalic lines and create interest while playing diatonically.

The second part of the phrase uses a Dm7 arpeggio and resolves to the 3rd (E) of Cmaj7. Over the Cmaj7 chord the lick continues with an E Minor Pentatonic scale run (this works well because it's like playing a substitution on the 3rd of the chord), before ending on the 7th (B) of Cmaj7. I find the easiest way to play this is with a pull-off and a slide, as illustrated below, but experiment to play it in a way that is comfortable for you.

This example might appear quite simple to play, but it is rich in harmonic information. I suggest taking some of the substitutions mentioned above, and practising them over a static chord, so that you can hear the different tensions they create, before moving on.

Example 1g

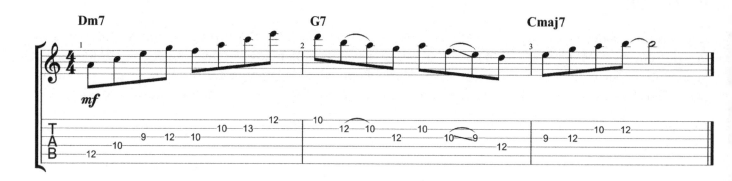

Example 1h uses the D Minor Pentatonic scale in bar one. This may seem an obvious choice to play over Dm7, but it can be used very effectively. Imagine the notes of D Minor Pentatonic as though they are an arpeggio and they spell a Dm7add11 chord:

D	F	G	A	C
1	3	11(or 4)	5	7

Over the G7 chord, the notes come from a Bm7b5 arpeggio. Remember that you don't always have to play arpeggios from their root – you can alter the sequence of the notes to create new melodies.

The line resolves over the Cmaj7 chord using a stack of 4ths to spell out the sound of a Cmaj7add13 chord which adds a slightly richer flavour. (We will discuss quartal harmony further in a moment).

Example 1h

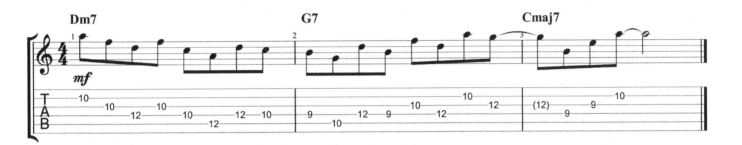

Bar one of Example 1i uses a "shell voicing" Fmaj7 arpeggio over the Dm7 chord, combined with a straight D minor triad.

A shell voicing is a chord voicing that use only the root, 3rd and 7th intervals. Jazz musicians often use just two notes to define the sound of a chord, such as root and 3rd, root and 7th, or 3rd and 7th without the root. Playing lines like this with no exotic ingredients forces us to dig deeper to create a strong melody.

Over the G7 chord, a simple scale run resolves to **the 3**rd (E) of Cmaj7. It's good to include some scale runs in your playing. These were the stock material of pre-Coltrane hardbop and bebop. After resolving to the E, there is another stack of 4ths and the lick ends on the 9th (D) of Cmaj7.

Example 1i

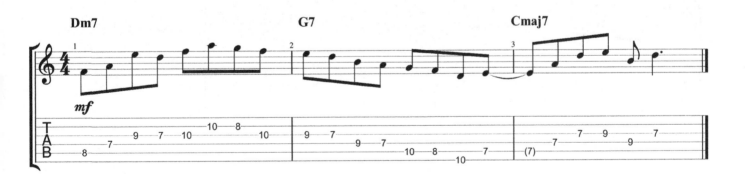

Traditionally, chords are formed by stacking intervals of a 3rd. For example, the notes C, E, G and B form Cmaj7. But it is also possible to stack chords in 4th intervals e.g. C, F, B and E. Stacking notes in 4ths is known as *quartal* harmony and was popularised in jazz by Miles Davis during his modal period.

Quartal harmony has a spaced-out, undefined quality evocative of modern jazz. (For a classic example of this, listen to pianist McCoy Tyner on John Coltrane's recordings. Early recordings of Herbie Hancock and Chick Corea made great use of quartal voicings too.

While many books could be devoted to its application, suffice to say that it is possible to replace most traditional jazz chords with quartal voicings.

The example below uses descending quartal voicings over the Dm7 chord. Over the G7 chord, the quartal voicings are separated by a G7 arpeggio. Remember, everything is still diatonic to the tonic C Major scale.

Example 1j

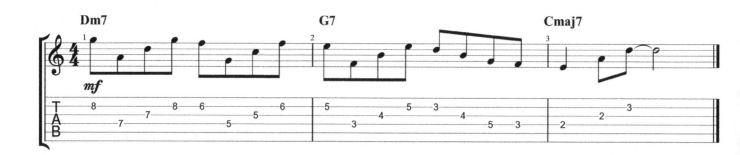

Example 1k uses a D minor triad followed by a scale run. A Bmb5 (1 b3 b5) shell voicing is played over the G7 chord. The line continues with a descending scale run that resolves to the 3rd of Cmaj7. The short line over the Cmaj7 is drawn from an Em7 arpeggio.

Example 1k

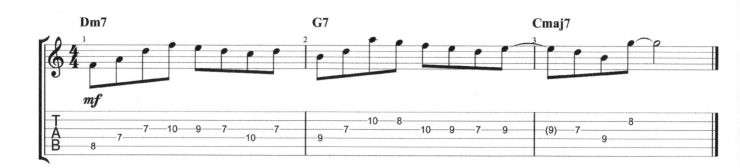

You can also play an arpeggio from the 5th degree of a chord. Example 1l uses an Am7 arpeggio over the Dm7 chord and combines it with an F major triad. Initially, the Am7 shape doesn't contain the 3rd, so still sounds like a D minor melody, but the F note is added later in the line.

The table below is an easy way to show how the notes / intervals of these three chords relate to one another on a minor 7 chord. Experiment by recording yourself playing a static chord, then improvising with all three arpeggios over the top.

What this table shows is that you can solo using Dm7, Fmaj7 and Am7 arpeggios over a Dm7 chord. The Fmaj7 and Am7 arpeggios add different extensions to your melodic lines. As you go further away from the original chord, the arpeggios have less in common with the underlying harmony. The most common arpeggio to use is the one on the 3rd (Fmaj7 in this case) which helps you access the 3-9 intervals.

Upper-structure arpeggios to play over Dm7

	1	3	5	7	9	11
Dm7	D	F	A	C		
FMaj7		F	A	C	E	
Am7			A	C	E	G

Over the G7 chord in Example 11 there is a cascading arpeggio idea that moves through Bm7b5 and G7 arpeggios (playing Bm7b5 over G7 is once again the arpeggio from the 3rd). Both are played in 1st inversion, so that the root is the highest note. The use of hammer-ons and the layout of the arpeggios makes this line easiest to play with a combination of legato and small sweeps. If you play the line using these techniques, you should be able to achieve the cascading effect even at faster tempi.

Example 11

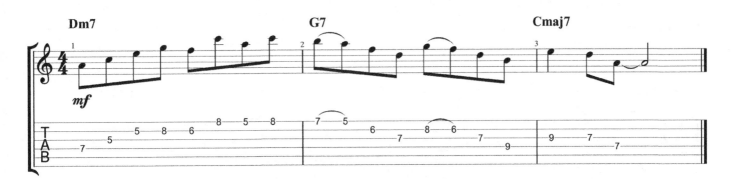

Example 1m begins with a Coltrane-esque "1 2 3 5" interval line that you must have in your vocabulary! It illustrates a practical way to turn a triad into a four-note pattern that spans half a bar.

The line continues with a quartal arpeggio from a G note. The quartal arpeggio is a good way to spell out a Dm11 sound, since it contains the 11th (G), 7th (C) and 3rd (F).

Over the G7 is an idea that outlines a G13 sound. It is constructed around a drop 2 voicing of the G13 chord shape, with an added note on each string – a technique that allows you to create a two note per string arpeggio. I suggest learning this shape and using it as a sound in its own right.

The line resolves to the 3rd (E) of Cmaj7, then ascends a quartal arpeggio.

Example 1m

The next examples uses a chord voicing of Dm7 and makes effective use of a small number of notes. This lick also demonstrates a common rule in counterpoint melody writing: to resolve a series of large ascending intervals with a stepwise movement in the opposite direction.

Not all counterpoint "rules" hold true for jazz, but many do and it's helpful to bear this in mind if you want to create strong melodies. This idea appears so often in Charlie Parker's playing that you might suspect he studied the topic!

In Example 1n, the line over the G7 emphasizes first a C note then, on beat 3, resolves this to a B to create a clear G7sus4 to G7 movement. The line continues with a G7 arpeggio inversion that resolves to the 3rd (E) of C.

Example 1n

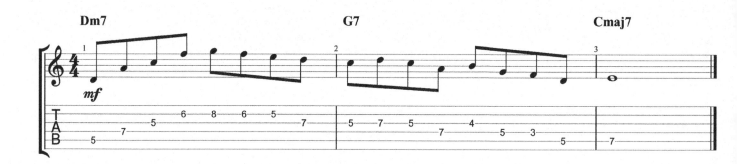

The final line in this chapter is placed higher on the fretboard to vary things a bit. It uses F major and A minor triad arpeggios over Dm7. The F major triad is played ascending, while the A minor triad follows a 3 1 5 3 pattern.

At the beginning of the second bar, I use a Dm7 arpeggio over the G7 chord, followed by a scale run, before the lines resolves to the 7th (B) of Cmaj7.

The table below shows how these arpeggios relate to one another. In Example 1n, I purposely chose to stay with the G7sus4 sound, however the line is more scalic and the note C resolves strongly to the B on the Cmaj7 chord.

Upper-structure arpeggios to play over G7

	1	3	5	7	9	11
G7	G	B	D	F		
Bm7(b5)		B	D	F	A	
Dm7			D	F	A	C

Example 1o

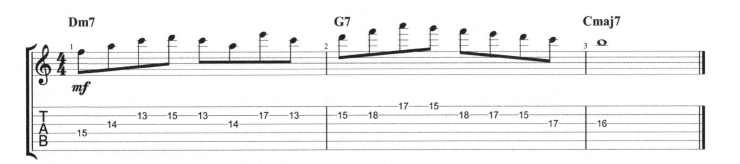

Practise using Dm7 over G7 by playing a static chord and superimposing the arpeggios listed in the table above. The only thing to watch for here is to choose carefully when to use the C note. Playing a C over a G7 chord will suggest a G7sus4 sound. This might be desirable in some instances but not in others.

Chapter Assignments

Write a set of five or more licks, or a short solo, over the II V I progression using:

- Triads or arpeggios chained together as shown in Example 1e

- Diatonic triads or arpeggios in sequences

- Triad inversions

- Using the arpeggio on the 3rd or 5th of the chord

- The pentatonic scale from the root of a II or VI minor chord, or the 3rd of the I chord (e.g., E Minor Pentatonic over Cmaj7

- Quartal shapes, chord voicings with added notes, or shell voicings

- Coltrane patterns (1 2 3 5 on a major chord, 1 b3 4 5 on a minor chord)

When you work with these ideas, remember to focus on the melody more than the arpeggio you're using. Experiment with different patterns, sequences and inversions and, of course, include things you know that are already part of your vocabulary. All these ideas will prove valuable when you apply them to the material in the rest of this book.

Chapter Two – Chromatic Enclosures

Using chromaticism is a wonderful way to add some bebop jazz flavour to your solos. In this chapter I'll explain how to add chromatic passing notes to the major scale and illustrate chromatic enclosures. Both techniques will help you capture the bebop / hardbop sound in your melodic lines.

The best way to think of chromaticism is as a technique used to highlight "target" notes. Chromatic notes are not scale notes, so in isolation they sound out of place. If, however, they are used to target a note that is in the scale, they are a great way to introduce tension and resolution. This is precisely why they appeal to our ears in solos: a chromatic note is a "surprise" that leads somewhere. We can hear that it needs to resolve and it satisfies our ears when it does!

Adding chromatic passing notes to a scale

To demonstrate this technique we will use the C Major scale shown in Example 2a below.

Example 2a – C Major scale

I have a method for adding in chromatic notes that may be a surprise to you, but it sounds good and it works. This method was taught to me by the jazz pianist Barry Harris, during one of his workshops at the Royal Conservatoire of The Hague.

Chromatic notes can be added between scale notes in this manner:

- If there is a whole-step interval between scale notes, play a half-step note in between. For example, add a G# between the notes G and A in the C Major scale

- If there is a half-step interval between scale notes, then play the scale note above the higher note. E.g. There is a half-step between E and F in the C Major scale, so add a G note – the note above F in the scale

This is illustrated in Example 2b

Example 2b – Two types of approach note

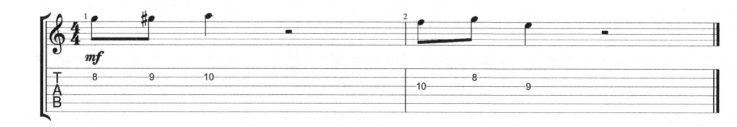

Taken to its logical conclusion, we can add a chromatic note between all the notes in the C Major scale. This means that we can we can play 1/8th note jazz lines that begin on a scale note and cause all the strong chord tones to fall on the beat, and the chromatic passing notes on the off-beat. This is useful, because in hardbop / bebop jazz, chromatic notes are generally placed on the off-beats.

Examples 2c and 2d show the C Major scale with chromatic notes inserted. It will be helpful for you to learn these patterns, but also to experiment with them and find different transition points and ways of adding the passing notes.

Thoughts on technique and phrasing

I tend to play these exercises using a legato technique with lots of hammer-ons, pull-offs and slides. Aim to pick a chromatic note and resolve it to the following note with a legato movement. This should result in nice phrasing, because the passing note is accented and the scale note is softer. To aid this approach, I try to keep passing notes and scale notes on the same string where possible.

Example 2c – Ascending C Major scale with approach notes

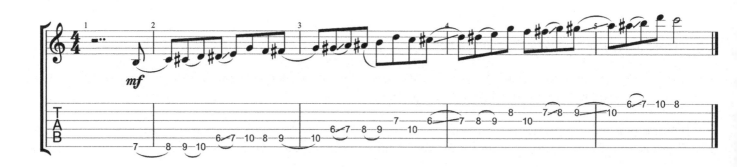

Example 2d – Descending C Major scale with approach notes

Two-note chromatic enclosures

A chromatic enclosure is a short phrase that mixes scale notes and chromatic passing notes to emphasise a target note. Think of it in these terms: you want to highlight one particular note, but surround it with other notes that lead to it. In jazz, enclosures can range in length anything from two to ten notes. This is a key part of Pat Metheny's style, and you will hear him fill entire bars with chromatic enclosures.

Let's look at some simple two-note enclosures. The concept is, for each note of a C major triad, to play a chromatic note below and a diatonic note above. Example 2e shows how this sounds for a C major triad in the 8th position.

The first two bars of this lick place the chromatic note first, followed by the diatonic note, then the triad note. The second two bars flip this sequence around – the diatonic note is played first, then the chromatic note, then the triad note. Either way sounds good, so you can find your preference.

Example 2e – Chromatic enclosures on a C major triad

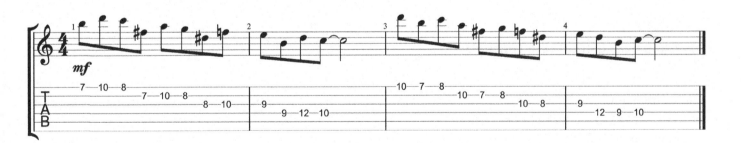

Now let's expand this idea to include the other two chords in our II V I sequence. Example 2f demonstrates chromatic enclosures for D minor and G major triads.

Example 2f – Chromatic enclosures on D minor and G major triads

Four-note chromatic enclosures

We can take this idea a step further with four-note enclosures. These are very common in modern jazz, since they provide an easy way to emphasise the basic jazz groove, in which the "heavy" beats fall on the 1 and the 3. With more notes to play with, there can be more permutations of the sequence. Example 2g illustrates five very common approaches.

Example 2g – Five examples of 4-note enclosures

Example licks using these concepts

Now here are ten lines that use the ideas discussed in this chapter. The first example uses the "passing note" chromaticism taught to me by Barry Harris. The first bar contains two passing notes over the Dm7 chord. A G note is placed between the F and E notes; an Eb is placed between the E and D. From there the line continues a descending Dm7 arpeggio – C to A. After the A note is played, an A# passing note is used to target the B that falls on beat 1 of the second bar. Over the G7 chord there is a B diminished triad, followed by the same passing note idea which resolves to an E note over the Cmaj7 chord.

Example 2h

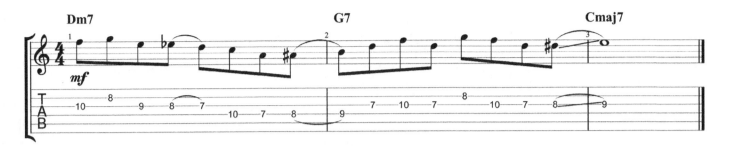

In the next example, an Am7 arpeggio and an F major 1 2 3 5 Coltrane pattern are played over the Dm7 chord. The use of the notes E and G from the Am7 arpeggio could be thought of as a chromatic enclosure.

Playing the arpeggio from the 5th degree of the minor seventh chord creates a nice sound over a II chord, but you could consider adding the 3rd of the Dm7 chord, since that note is not in the arpeggio. Adding the third helps to clearly define the sound of the underlying chord.

Chromatic passing notes are put to use over the G7 chord. Starting on a D note at the 10th fret, chromatic notes target the B note on beat 3. From the B onwards, the rest of the bar is a descending G7 arpeggio. The last two notes neatly encircle the 3rd of Cmaj7 (E). A permutation of the 1 2 3 5 Coltrane pattern is played over the Cmaj7 chord.

Example 2i

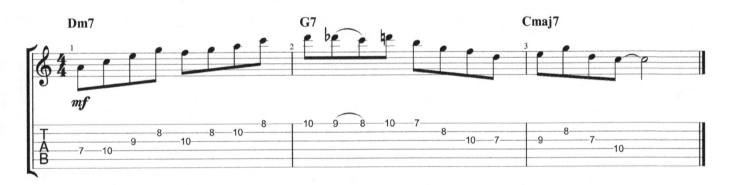

Playing an arpeggio from the 3rd of a chord is a useful device to produce characteristic bebop lines. The following example uses an Fmaj7 arpeggio in bar one, built off the 3rd degree of the Dm7 chord. A passing note at the end of the bar leads into bar two to target a B note, which is the 3rd of the G7 chord. The rest of the second bar is a G7 arpeggio that skips up to the 9th of the chord (A) via a chromatic passing note and resolves to the 3rd of Cmaj7. The line concludes with a short diatonic melody that ends on the 7th of Cmaj7 (B).

Example 2j

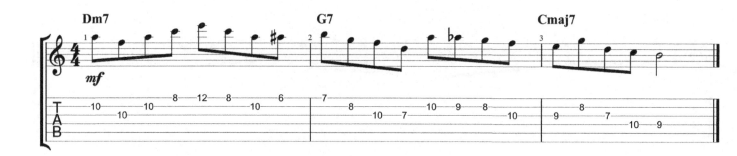

The Dm7 line in the next example is a scale run from the 5th down to the 7th of the Dm7 chord, with a passing note added between the F and E. Since it's not possible to add a chromatic note in between, I added a G note (the diatonic note above F). Listen to how natural that approach sounds.

The transition to G7 is made with a two-note enclosure. C and A# notes encircle the B that falls on beat 1 of bar two. The line continues with another enclosure that targets a D note – the 5th of G7. From the D the line follows a 1 2 3 5 pattern; a passing Ab note leads into a G over the Cmaj7 chord (the 5th of Cmaj7). The short melody at the end uses notes from an Em7 arpeggio.

Example 2k

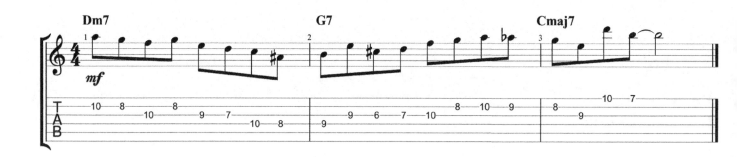

Starting an ascending scale run with a two-note enclosure is a great way to break up phrase that is essentially a scale run. In bar one, the melody is a scale run from D to A, but the D is preceded with an E and C# enclosure.

The movement to G7 is achieved with a passing Ab. Over the G7 chord there is a G7 arpeggio with an E note added between the F and D. Before the low B at the end of the bar there is another two-note enclosure adding a C and A#.

Resolving to the 5th (G) of Cmaj7, the melody comes to rest via a scale run down to the 3rd (E).

Example 2l

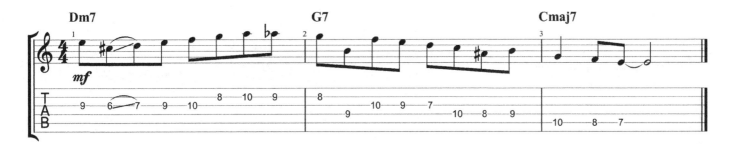

Example 2m uses the two-note enclosure in several places. First, it encircles the F note over the Dm7 in bar one, again breaking up a predictable scale run. At the end of the bar, C and A notes are used to encircle the B over the G7 chord. The line skips from B to D, then descends the scale adding a D# to target the 3rd (E) of Cmaj7 using an F and D# enclosure.

The final part of the lick over the Cmaj7 contains another enclosure that targets the 5th (G) with an A and an F#.

Example 2m

Four-note enclosures can work in two ways. They can precede a chord tone to create a suspended sound, or they can be used as a way of "pulling" towards the chord tone you intend to resolve to.

In Example 2n, the Dm7 line uses the first of these approaches. The Fmaj7 arpeggio beginning on beat 3 is suspended by the chromatic enclosure that fills the first half of the bar.

This line leads into the G7 bar by encircling the note D (5th). The first part of the line in bar two is a fragment of G Major Pentatonic, which is followed by another enclosure. The second approach then comes into play as the enclosure creates a tension that pulls towards a resolving note over Cmaj7.

Example 2n

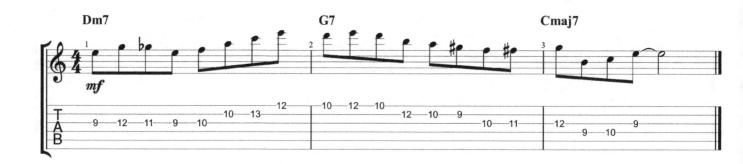

The next line uses a descending Dm7 arpeggio that moves into a chromatic enclosure targeting an F (7th of G). Over the G7 chord, the line continues with an Fmaj7 arpeggio inversion. The result is to create a G7sus4 sound. This is followed by a clichéd G7 passing note phrase.

You may already be familiar with the latter bebop line. Analysed with the Barry Harris method, it is a scale run from G to E. A Gb is inserted between G and F, and a G between F and E. This part of the lick ends on an E that resolves to the Cmaj7.

Over the Cmaj7, the melody continues with a fragment of the E Blues scale. In this context, the blue note (A#) works as a chromatic passing note between A and B.

Example 2o

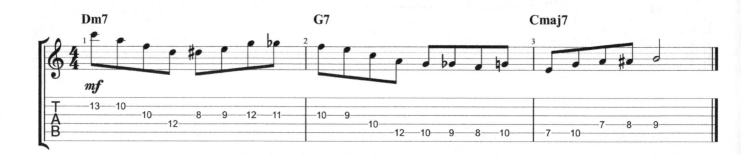

Example 2p opens with a chromatic enclosure reminiscent of Pat Metheny's chromatic lines. (Pat used chromatics extensively around the time of his *Question and Answer* album). From the enclosure, the line moves on into a 1 2 3 5 D minor pattern, in this case played descending.

The line played over the G7 chord is constructed by combining the E Minor Pentatonic scale with a chromatic enclosure that targets a D note (9th of Cmaj7). This is another example of how an enclosure can create tension that pulls towards a resolution over the I chord. The line ends with a descending Em7 arpeggio over Cmaj7.

Example 2p

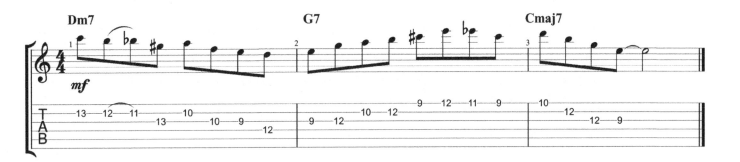

The final example of this chapter illustrates what happens when an enclosure is moved away from the strong beats of the bar. In bar one, two-note enclosures encircle the root and 3rd of Dm7. Notice how this breaks up the arpeggio. The American pianist Charlie Banacos taught this approach, which influenced the styles of Mike Stern and Michael Brecker, among others. This is an interesting idea to explore, even if it ignores the key of C Major a little bit!

The line in bar two starts on the 3rd of G7 (B) and moves to the 5th (D), clearly spelling out the G7 sound. The chromatic enclosure in this bar is placed on beat 2, so that it will resolve on beat 4 of the bar. This leaves a chromatic note on beat 3, which is a strong beat in jazz. The effect is to give the line an unresolved quality, again reminiscent of Metheny. Using this idea throughout a solo can open things up, because the melodic lines will sound less connected to the underlying chords, achieving a more modern sound.

Example 2q

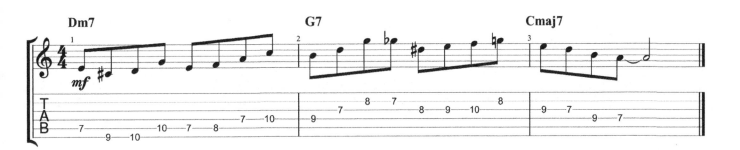

Chapter Assignments

Write a set of five or more licks over a progression, or a short solo, using:

- Chromatic passing notes. Try to apply this to other scales, such as the harmonic minor, or a chord sound that I didn't cover

- Experiment with two-note enclosures and make use of the fact that they create a natural flow of three-note groupings to break up the rhythmic flow

- Focus on using the enclosures to suspend the sound of a chord

- Focus on using the enclosures to create tension that helps transition to the next chord

- Experiment combining two- and four-note enclosures to create longer, more "open" sounding structures that have more rhythmic freedom

Chromatic enclosures and passing notes are a big part of the sound we associate with the bebop and hardbop melodic language. However, be careful to exercise some control over how you use them: remain aware that their main purpose is to target or gravitate towards scale / chord tones.

Chapter Three – Harmonic Minor on the V

So far we have explored the unaltered major scale and added chromatic passing notes to create more tension and resolution. The next place to explore, to take our improvisation over the II V I to a higher level is the harmonic minor scale, which can be a rich source of melodic choices.

The jazz standards we play were, for the most part, written by classically trained composers in the tradition of the Romantic period. Many of the harmonic devices used are similar to those used by Chopin, Schubert and Berlioz – so listening to classical music alongside jazz can teach us a lot about both styles. Historically, jazz harmony is the combination of Romantic Harmony with an added twist, achieved by mixing it with the Blues.

All the examples below will be in the key of F Major and the dominant V chord would normally be a straight C7. However, we will borrow the dominant seventh chord from the F Harmonic Minor scale which extends to become a C7b9b13.

Normally, when playing over the C7 chord in the key of F, most guitarists would be "thinking" C Mixolydian (the fifth mode of the major scale), however, as we are borrowing the C7b9b13 chord from F Harmonic Minor, we can access some more interesting sounds. It makes sense that we can use the fifth mode of the Harmonic minor scale to solo over this chord. Some people call this scale C Mixolydian b9 b13, but *Phrygian Dominant* is a common name as it has the same intervals as Phrygian, but with a major 3rd.

The table below compares the C Mixolydian scale (F Major played from the 5th degree) to C Phrygian Dominant (F Harmonic Minor scale played from the 5th degree).

C Mixolydian	C	D	E	F	G	A	Bb
C Mixolydian(b9, b13)	C	Db	E	F	G	Ab	Bb

The straight C Mixolydian mode gives us some nice extended notes to improvise with – the 9th (D), 11th (F) and 13th (A). But the modal scale produced by the harmonic minor contains a b9 (Db) and a b13 (Ab) – notes that create tension and pull more strongly towards a resolution. This makes the scale ideal for creating more tension and interest over our II V I progression. It produces a sound that people don't expect to hear. Let's look at the F Harmonic Minor scale in the 8th position.

Example 3a – Harmonic minor

The augmented 2nd interval between the notes Db and E is a stretch and can make this scale a bit difficult to play in a three note per string pattern, so play through the example above slowly. Also try playing it in thirds to embed the sound in your head and learn where the intervals fall.

Take care to learn the notes you are playing and not just the pattern. If you know the notes, later you will find it much easier to compose lines using the scale, and you will understand which notes in the scale relate to the chords you are improvising over.

When you are familiar with the sound of scale, the next step is to consider the triads that it produces. This will yield more material to use when creating melodic lines. Example 3b demonstrates the diatonic triads of F Harmonic Minor, written as a scale exercise. Playing through this will be of immense help in creating interesting melodic ideas, so it doesn't sound as though you're simply running up and down scales. Solos that only contain 1/8th scalic ideas get boring pretty quickly!

Example 3b – Harmonic minor triads

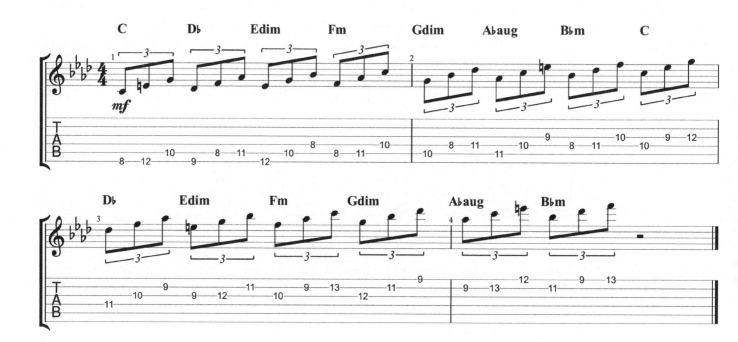

We can develop this idea further by doing the same exercise with diatonic 7th chords, creating arpeggios.

Example 3c – Harmonic minor diatonic arpeggios

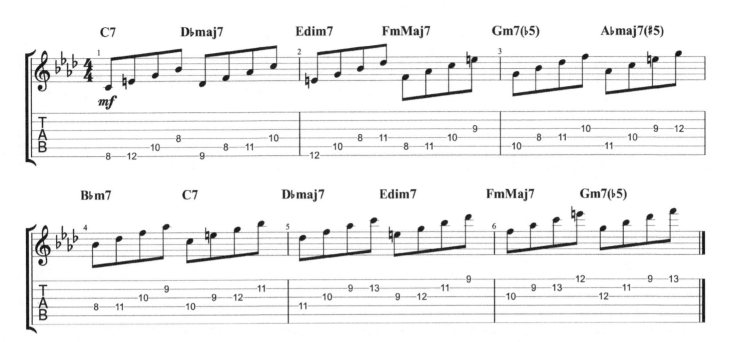

Having played through all of the arpeggios above, you can probably hear the ones that will be most useful when playing over a C7 chord. This doesn't mean you can't use any of the other arpeggios, but the ones I have selected below will convey a C7 (b9, b13) sound. The arpeggios I recommend are:

- Cmaj

- Edim

- Gdim

- Abaug

- Bbdim

- C7

- Edim

- Abmaj7#5

Example 3d – Useful arpeggios to play over C7

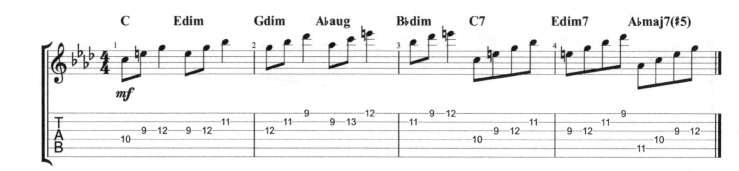

Example lines using these concepts

Let's hear how these concepts sound in practice. Example 3e uses a simple Gm7 arpeggio, preceded by a beautiful enclosure of the root. It means that the root falls on the "2-and" beat, which makes it more rhythmically interesting. The rest of the line uses only Gm7 arpeggio notes and encircles a C note (the 3rd of Fmaj7). The dominant 7th line is a scale run drawn from the harmonic minor, emphasising the b9. This is followed by a C7 arpeggio. It resolves to the 5th of Fmaj7, using the b9 to create some tension.

Example 3e

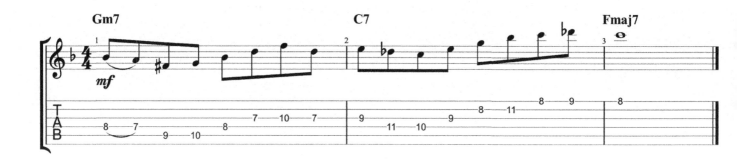

One of the melodic counterpoint rules commonly used in bebop is that a large interval in one direction is best resolved with a stepwise motion in the opposite direction. This is illustrated in Example 3f. The line opens with a skip from the root of the Gm7 chord to the fifth, then descends to an A note on beat 3. Next you may spot the familiar Coltrane 1 3 4 5 minor pattern from an A to a D note.

The dominant 7th line in this example uses a common "trick" – which is to add in the #9 as well as the b9. In this instance the #9 is an Eb, which sounds great over the C7 chord. It functions a bit like a chromatic passing note, as it leads nicely to E – the 3rd of C7. The line is resolved by a descending scale run to the 3rd of Fmaj7 (A).

Example 3f

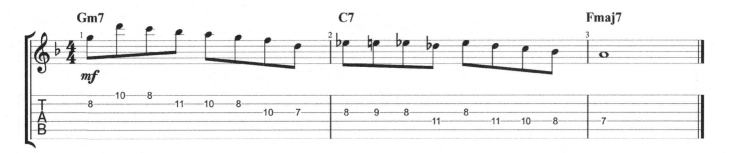

In the next example, the lick played over the Gm7 encloses the chord tone with a diatonic note above and a chromatic note below. The same idea is applied first to the root, then the 3rd.

The line over the C7 chord descends in diatonic thirds from E, then ascends an Ab augmented triad that resolves nicely to a G note, suggesting an Fmaj9 chord.

Example 3g

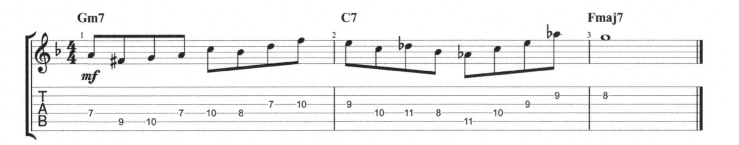

Example 3h begins with two arpeggios: a stack of 4ths starting on a C note, followed by a Bbmaj7 arpeggio. Over the C7 chord there is an E diminished arpeggio – the main arpeggio associated with this type of jazz – played as an inversion beginning on G.

Notice that the transition from Gm7 to C7 is accomplished with a motif. The descending Bbmaj7 arpeggio motif is repeated using the descending E diminished arpeggio. This is a different approach to moving from one chord to the next by targeting chord tones. It's good to have both motif-based and target note ideas in your arsenal of lines.

The resolution from C7 to Fmaj7 comes via a chromatic enclosure of an A note – the 3rd of Fmaj7.

Example 3h

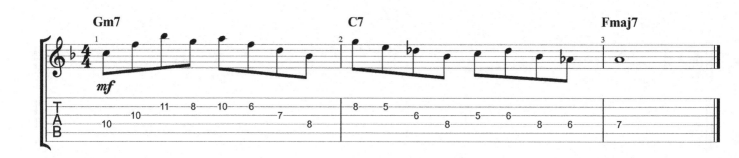

In the next example the first note is a passing note leading to the 3rd of Gm7. From there it follows a descending Gm7 arpeggio. The line applies the rule that a large intervallic skip should be balanced with a stepwise movement in the opposite direction – but this time it is a descending arpeggio, rather than a scale movement.

The line played over C7 makes use of the Ab augmented triad (from the earlier list of recommended choices) and combines it with an E diminished arpeggio. The top notes of the two forms move in a stepwise direction and connect the melody to the C7 chord. The low Db in the diminished arpeggio resolves naturally to its neighbouring C – the 5th of Fmaj7.

Example 3i

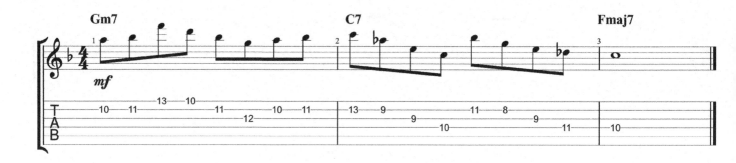

Playing an arpeggio from the 5th of the II chord is a fantastic way to target the third of the V chord that follows it. To the ears, it sounds like a suspended chord, but without moving very far from the key. The line over the Gm7 descends stepwise to the 3rd of C7.

The line over the C7 chord begins with an E diminished arpeggio and continues with a C7 arpeggio. The line resolves by the Ab note moving up a semitone to A – the 3rd of Fmaj7.

Example 3j

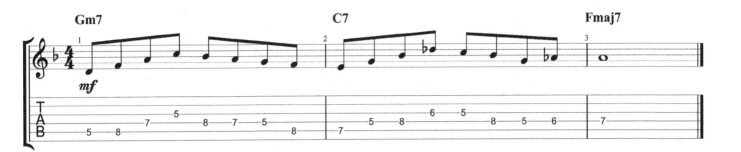

A useful concept to bring more variation to your melodic lines is to use triads arranged in different patterns. Example 3k begins with a G minor triad played in a 3 1 3 5 sequence. It continues into a quartal arpeggio leading from a G note, using the same pattern. The effect is to create a repeating motif.

This time over the C7 chord we have a Bbm7b5 arpeggio. Strictly speaking, Bbm7b5 is not a diatonic chord of F Harmonic Minor, but it is possible to construct this arpeggio with notes from the scale. Below this is illustrated by showing the F Harmonic Minor scale played from Bb.

F Harmonic Minor (from Bb)	Bb	C	Db	E	F	G	Ab
Bbm7	Bb		Db		F		Ab
Bbm7b5	Bb		Db	E			Ab

Using Bbm7b5 over the C7 chord imposes the intervals of the b7, b9, 3 and #5. They sound great!

Some great lines can be created by looking at the notes in a scale and seeing what other arpeggios can be constructed by stacking 3rds (a topic I'll return to in the altered and diminished scale chapters later in the book).

Here, the Bbm7b5 arpeggio continues into an Ab augmented triad, which resolves to the 3rd (A) of Fmaj7.

Example 3k

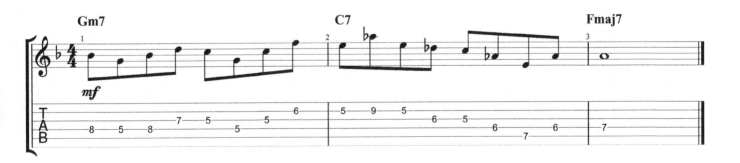

Over a II chord, a common bebop device is to approach the third chromatically from a whole step above. In the example below this is the chromatic descent from C to Bb.

The line played over the C7 chord is constructed with G diminished and Ab augmented triads. Pairing triads like this creates a very strong melodic structure, and is a familiar sound to our ears. Modern jazz saxophonists such as George Garzone and Michael Brecker often solo using pairs of triads that have no notes in common, which creates an angular, unresolved sound. Here I am using the G diminished triad in root position and Ab augmented in first inversion. The line resolves to the 9th (G) of Fmaj7.

Example 3l

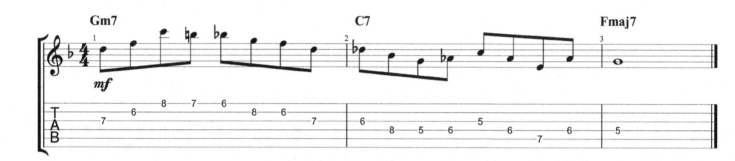

The next line uses a Dm7 arpeggio over the II chord which targets to 3rd of Gm7 (Bb). It then skips to a D note to descend the scale. This movement allows the line to end neatly on the b13 (Ab) of C7. The b13 really emphasises the dominant sound borrowed from F Harmonic Minor.

The line over the C7 chord uses the more exotic Abmaj7#5(9) arpeggio, which continues up to the 11th (Db). From there an ascending chromatic approach is used to resolve to the 5th (C) of Fmaj7.

Example 3m

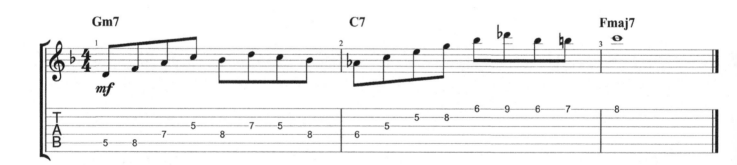

In the final example of this chapter I'll demonstrate another way of using a Dm7 arpeggio on the Gm7 chord. This time I have omitted the 3rd (Bb) of Gm7 which immediately makes the line more open sounding. In isolation, it could sound like a G7sus4 chord, but is fine when we hear it in the context of our key of F Major. We can play challenging lines like this as long as we are conscious of their overall effect on the music.

On the C7 chord, the line is made up of a pair of diatonic 3rds, then a C7#5 arpeggio. The latter is another useful arpeggio that is not diatonic to F Harmonic Minor, but can be constructed from a C7 triad with an added augmented 5th.

Example 3n

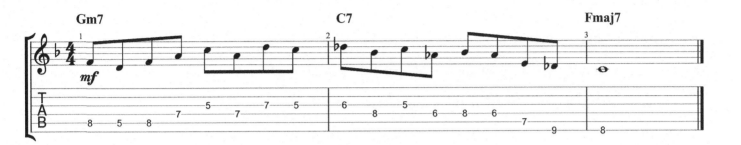

Chapter Assignments

Write a set of five or more licks over a progression, or a short solo, using:

- The diminished arpeggio built on the 3rd of the V chord (E diminished over C7 in the examples)

- Experiment with some of the triad pairs that clearly convey the harmonic minor sound. E.g. Gdim, Abaug, C and Db

- Write some lines using the C7#5 arpeggio

- Over the II chord, play the pentatonic scale from the root of the II or VI chord

- Create some licks using the Bbm7b5 arpeggio over the C7

As always, focus on the melody more than the type of arpeggio you're using.

Chapter Four – Altered Scale

The altered scale is the seventh mode of the melodic minor scale and one of the most commonly used when soloing over dominant chords. Typically used over an altered dominant chord, it creates an "outside" sound which is then resolved when the progression moves to the I chord.

If you are new to improvising with the altered scale, initially it can be challenging to make melodic sense of it. We don't tend to think in terms of altered extensions and often have no real idea what they sound like! In this chapter we will look at some arpeggios extracted from the altered scale that work well over altered dominant chords. The examples will not only help you get used to the sound, but provide you with clear examples of how to compose strong melodic lines.

We will work in the key of Eb Major, so all the examples will be played over Bb7alt (the dominant chord of Eb) using the Bb Altered scale.

Example 4a – Bb Altered scale

The Bb Altered scale is the seventh mode of B Melodic Minor, so let's examine the triads and arpeggios we can use in terms of B Minor, for the sake of simplicity.

First, here are the diatonic triads:

Example 4b – Diatonic triads

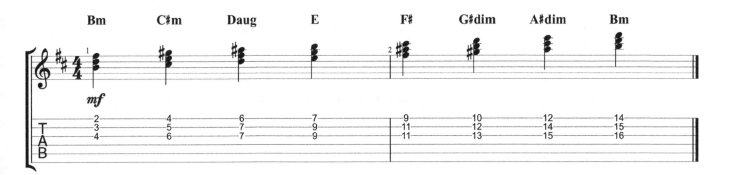

As in previous chapters, we can extend these to form diatonic 7th arpeggios.

Example 4c – Diatonic 7th arpeggios

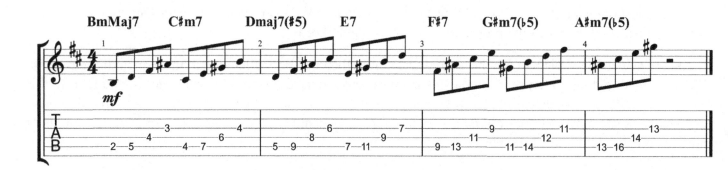

The hunt for a good diatonic arpeggio!

Even though we want to play this scale over a Bb dominant chord, notice that there is no Bb7 diatonic arpeggio in the scale. In fact, the tonic chord is a Bbm7b5 so there is no obvious go-to arpeggio that outlines a dominant sound. But, we can fix this.

The defining tones of a Bb7alt chord are the 3rd and 7th (F and Ab), so if we use arpeggios from the Bb Altered scale that contain those intervals we can stay close to the dominant sound and introduce some cool altered extensions. Only two chords contain both notes: E7 and G#m7b5. (G# = Ab)

E7 is the tritone substitute of Bb7.

G#m7b5 is related to E7, as it can be viewed as an arpeggio built on the 3rd of E7. Of the two options, the G#m7b5 arpeggio is probably the best candidate to spell out a Bb7alt sound.

The table below shows which intervals of Bb7alt are highlighted when you play a G#m7b5 arpeggio:

Arpeggio Note	G#	B	D	F#
Relative to Bb	b7	b9	3	b13

If you already know some different voicings of a Bb7alt chord, it's very likely that one of them is simply G#m7b5 with a Bb in the bass.

Quartal arpeggios and shell voicings can provide further melodic choices. Below I have written them out on the middle strings (D, G and B strings), and show them as chords rather than arpeggios, so it is clear how they are grouped together.

Example 4d – Diatonic quartal arpeggios on the middle string set

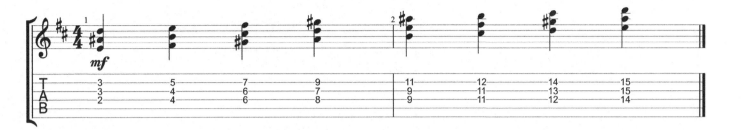

The same applies to shell voicings. A shell voicing consists of the root and defining 3rd and 7th intervals of a chord. An E7 shell voicing would therefore be E, G# and D. I have also written these as chords using the middle string set, but you should play through them both as chords and as arpeggios.

Example 4e – Diatonic shell voicings on the middle string set

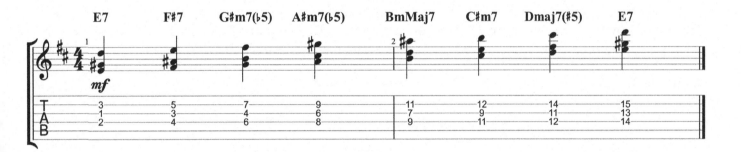

Examples of altered dominant lines

Now we have explored some concepts for improvising over the altered dominant chord, we can translate these into melodic examples over a II V7alt I progression. We are working in the key of Eb Major, so our chord progression is Fm7, Bb7alt, Ebmaj7.

The first example below highlights the sound of the chords using fairly simple devices. The Fm7 chord is spelt out with a descending Fm7 arpeggio. A scale run transitions the melody into the Bb7alt section. Over the Bb7alt chord there is an Abm7b5 arpeggio, followed by a small fragment that emphasises the b9 and #9 before it resolves to the 5th (Bb) of Ebmaj7.

Over the Ebmaj7 chord, the final notes come from a G minor triad. (Notice that I am referring to the G#m7b5 chord as Abm7b5. It's exactly the same chord, but makes more sense enharmonically, when related to a Bb dominant chord).

Example 4f

Using triplets to play 7th arpeggios is a great bebop trick that works well in a more modern jazz context as well. Example 4g begins with an Abmaj7 arpeggio over the Fm7, preceded by a leading note inserted before the root. The melody emphasises the top note of the arpeggio (G) which is the 9th of the Fm7 chord, then it descends a C minor arpeggio using the Coltrane pattern.

The line played over the Bb7alt is built from a Dmaj7#5 arpeggio, followed by a scale run that resolves to the 3rd (G) of Ebmaj7. Over the Ebmaj7 chord the melody is a fragment of a G Minor Pentatonic scale. Playing the minor pentatonic scale from the 3rd is a great device to use over tonic major chords.

Example 4g

Example 4h uses a shell voicing as an arpeggio. The line begins on the 5th of Fm7 and comes from an F minor descending triad. The 5th is followed by the 3rd of Fm7, then comes a two-note enclosure of the root note.

From the root note I spell out the F minor shell voicing which leads into the Bb7alt chord. Over the Bb7alt the line is based on an Abdim triad beginning on a D and skipping down to Bb. It returns to D, then descends the scale to resolve to the 3rd (G) of Ebmaj7. Over the Ebmaj7 the line skips from G to D and ends on the 6th (C) of Ebmaj7.

Example 4h

The next example takes an Fm7 arpeggio played from the 3rd of the chord. The line starts with a scale run from Eb up to G and, from there, down the Abmaj7 arpeggio. The line then transitions to a Bb note for the Bb7alt. The Bb is used as a leading note for a 2nd inversion E major triad. The line continues into a melody constructed from a F#sus4 triad and uses an Ab to resolve to Bb over the Ebmaj7. The melody over the Ebmaj7 chord is a G minor triad followed by an F – the 9th of Ebmaj7.

Example 4i

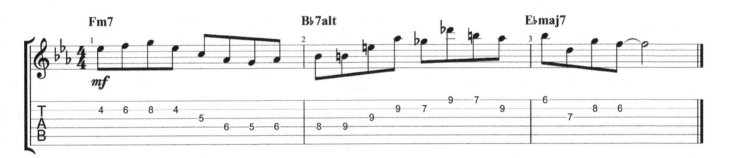

Suggesting passing chords that aren't written is a great way to create motion towards a chord change. In Example 4j, the line in bar one begins with an Fm7 arpeggio line. In bar two there is an Abm7b5 arpeggio played over the Bb7alt chord. To connect these two ideas, in the latter half of bar one we have a Gm7 arpeggio. The effect is a strong motion from the Fm7 to Bb7alt chords.

The Bb7alt line continues using a motif of diatonic thirds to resolve to the G over the Ebmaj7. The line ends on a F note, the 9th of Ebmaj7.

Example 4j

The beginning of this next example is a beautiful way of adding chromatic notes that connect arpeggio notes. In bar one, the addition of chromatic passing notes serves to embellish this Fm9 arpeggio. The use of 1/16th notes makes the rhythm more interesting.

From the last F note of bar one, the line moves up a semitone to Gb, then skips up to D and makes a small scale run to target a B on beat 3. The latter half of bar two is a simple B minor triad, but played over a Bb7alt chord creates b9 (B), 3rd (D) and b13 (Gb) intervals. The high B resolves to a Bb over the Ebmaj7 and the line ends on a D via an Eb passing note.

Example 4k

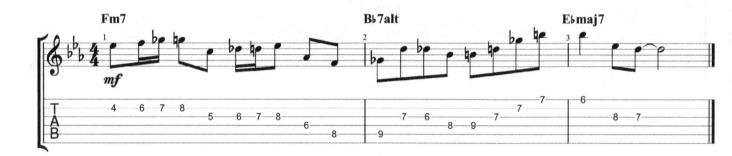

Lines can be made more interesting by introducing rhythmic variation. In the next example, an 8th note triplet is used for the chromatic passing notes that introduce the melody. A two-note enclosure follows that targets an Ab note on beat 3, then the line descends a C minor triad.

The line over the Bb7alt chord uses two arpeggios to ascend – Bm(maj7) and Abm7b5 – and ends on an F note over the Ebmaj7. This is followed by a scale fragment that returns to the F.

Example 4l

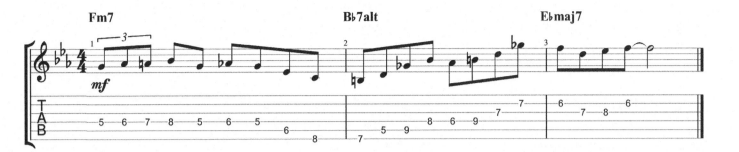

The line in bar one of Example 4m is a scale run that encloses the Ab target note then descends to C. Over the Bb7alt chord a 16th note trill is played that targets a D note. From the D the line descends the scale to B. The final three notes spell a D augmented triad that neatly resolves to the 9th (F) of Ebmaj7. The resolution of augmented triads is a common bop trait that has carried over into more modern styles. In this instance it is achieved by resolving the b13 (Gb) to F.

Example 4m

Example 4n opens with a simple F minor triad, rearranged in a 5 1 3 5 pattern, followed by a descending scale run. An E7 arpeggio, from the root down to the 3rd, is played over the Bb7alt chord to create a flat 5th sound. The line shifts into an E triad before resolving to the 3rd (G) of Eb.

Example 4n

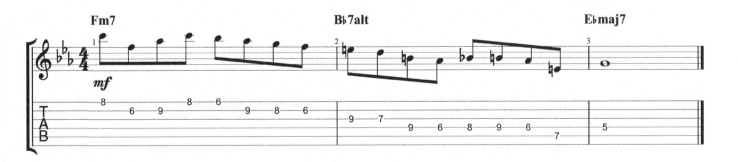

The final example of this chapter begins with a four-note chromatic enclosure (discussed in Chapter Two). In Example 4o the purpose of the enclosure is to suspend the 3rd of the Fm7 chord until beat 3, before the line continues with an Abmaj7 arpeggio. The line played over the Bb7alt chord is constructed by fusing together Dmaj7#5 and Bm(maj7) arpeggios. The line resolves from B to Bb on the first beat of bar three. The final two notes (G and F) convey the sound of an Ebmaj7(9) chord.

Example 4o

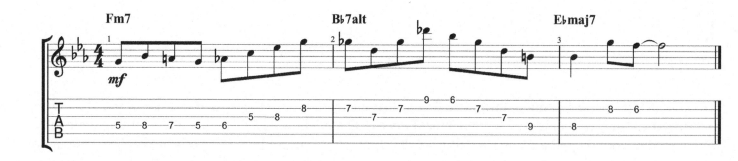

Chapter Assignments

Write a set of five or more licks over a progression, or create a short solo using:

- An Abm7b5 arpeggio over the Bb7alt chord

- Compose some lines using E7-based arpeggio variations – the tritone of Bb7 – and listen to how they work as Bb7 altered lines. Pay special attention to how the E note functions in this context

- Experiment with Dmaj7 shell voicings played over the Bb7alt chord

- Try fusing together different arpeggios over Bb7alt in order to come up with new lines

- Take the chromatic leading note idea from Example 4k and apply it to Bb7alt and Ebmaj7 lines, connecting the chord tones

Chapter Five – Diminished Scale on the Dom7th Chord

The half-whole diminished scale is a fairly recent addition to Western music. Though it appeared in earlier works, it didn't become a common device until the late 18th century. It is an eight note scale with a symmetrical, almost "mathematical" construction that in many ways sets it apart from tonal music and functional harmony. Luckily, we don't care too much about that in jazz – we are just concerned with whether it sounds good or not! In many different musical contexts the diminished scale is an effective means of adding colour and tension.

The diminished scale can be viewed as two interlocking diminished 7th chords that repeat symmetrically in minor 3rd intervals. One of the best ways to use a "synthetic" scale like this is to pick out and isolate the triads it contains. In this chapter we will use triads from the diminished scale to create lines over the dominant 7th chord in our II V I progression. All the musical examples are in the key of Bb Major, so our II V I progression is Cm7 (II), F7 (V), Bbmaj7 (I).

First, let's take a closer look at how to extract some useful diminished arpeggios.

Constructing the Diminished Scale

The Half Whole Diminished scale can be constructed from two diminished arpeggios a semitone apart. To construct an F Half Whole Diminished scale, you combine F diminished and Gb diminished arpeggios.

F Diminished: F Ab B D

Gb Diminished: Gb A C Eb

Arranged in order of pitch from F, this gives us the eight notes of the F Half Whole Diminished scale: F Gb Ab A B C D Eb F

As a formula, the diminished scale is 1 b9 #9 3 b5 5 6 b7

One way to play this scale is shown in Example 5a

Example 5a – Diminished scale:

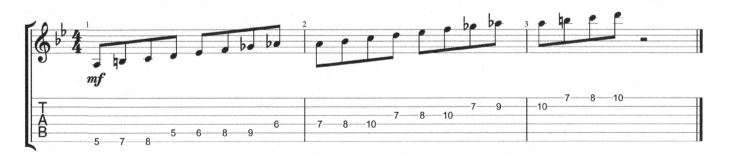

To discover what other arpeggios are hidden in the scale and available to us to use as soloing ideas, we can use the symmetrical aspect of the scale. Due to the nature of its construction using diminished arpeggios, everything that exists inside the Half Whole Diminished scale can be moved in minor 3rds, so we only have to look at the chords we can build on the first two notes (in this case F and Gb) and we can find the rest by transposing them in minor 3rd intervals.

Building chords from the F gives us these chords:

F	F	A	C	
Fm	F	Ab	C	
F(b5)	F	A	B	
Fdim	F	Ab	B	
F7	F	A	C	Eb
Fm7	F	Ab	C	Eb
F7(b5)	F	A	B	Eb
Fdim7	F	Ab	B	Eb

These chords are also shown in Example 5b.

Example 5b – Triads and 7th chords built from F in the diminished scale:

Building chords from the next note, Gb, is a little simpler:

Gbdim	Gb	A	C	
Gbdim7	Gb	A	C	Eb
Gbdim(Maj7)	Gb	A	C	F

These chords are shown in Example 5c.

Example 5c – Triads and 7th chords built from Gb in the diminished scale:

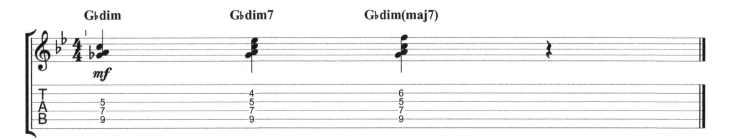

Now we have an overview of the different arpeggios or chords that are contained in the scale. Don't forget that they are also found on the other scale degrees – the arpeggios for F are also found on Ab, B and D. The Gb chords are also found on A, C and Eb.

Since the scale is being put to use over an F7 chord, it's helpful to know how the different notes relate to an F root, shown in the table below:

F	Gb	Ab	A	B	C	D	Eb
1	b9	#9	3	#11	5	13	b7

This scale contains rich extensions such as the b9, #9 and 13th. A dominant chord constructed with every extension would be an F13b9#11, although this would be a F7b5 if the C (5th) is omitted.

The most common sound associated with this scale is probably the 13b9. Guitarists generally think of this as an upper-structure triad placed above a dominant 7th chord. E.g. F713b9 is a D major triad over an F7 chord, spelt F A C Eb D Gb A.

A few rootless voicings of F13b9 are shown in Example 5d.

Example 5d – Diminished voicings

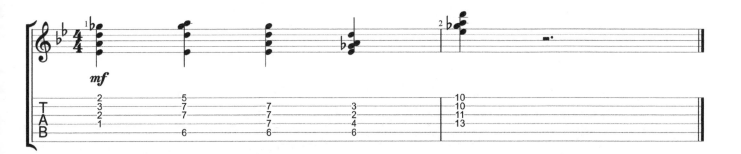

Triads

This chapter will focus on using major triads to create the diminished sound. The four major triads are F, Ab, B and D. Below are a few exercises to help you work on these triads and their inversions, and to help you connect them together to create your own lines.

In Exercise 5e, I have written out the triads across string sets, but in the same inversion.

Example 5e – 2nd inversion triads

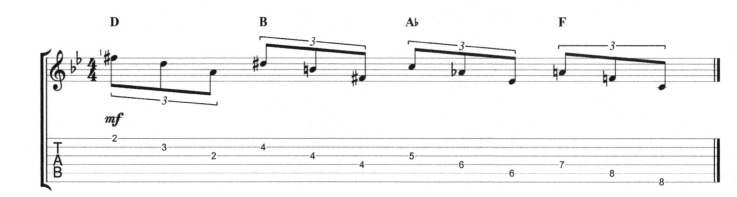

Example 5f – Root position triads

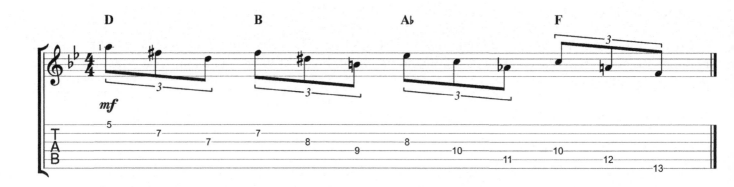

Example 5g – 1st inversion triads

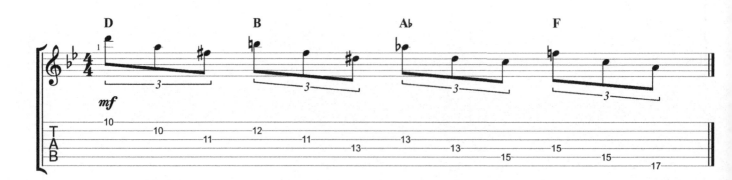

Another way to practise these triads is to mix and match the inversions, but play in the same position. Example 5h demonstrates cycling through the triads in a single position before moving to the next position to cycle through them again. All the triads are played on the D, G and B strings.

Example 5h – cycling through triads in inversions up the neck

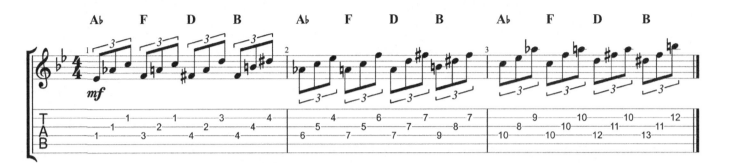

Example 5i shows one way to connect the triads together in order to improvise across the neck. Exercises like this are a great way to test your ability to locate the next triad in the sequence and create a melody that makes sense.

Example 5i – Improvised connection of triad inversions

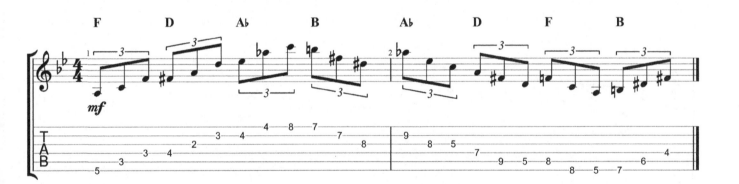

Examples of diminished scale lines

Now that we have some arpeggio and triad ideas to work with, we can put them to use to create melodic II V I lines.

Example 5j begins with a line that combines a Cm7 arpeggio with a quartal arpeggio built from the 5th (G) of the Cm7 chord.

For the F7 chord, the diminished line is played using a second inversion Ab major triad and a root position D major triad. The line resolves to the 3rd (D) of Bbmaj7 with a short scale run.

The combination of the Ab and D major triads conveys the sound of an F7 with a #9 (Ab), b9 (Gb) and 13 (D). The melody between the Ab and the D creates a voice leading transition between the two, as the Ab moves to A and the Eb moves to D.

Example 5j

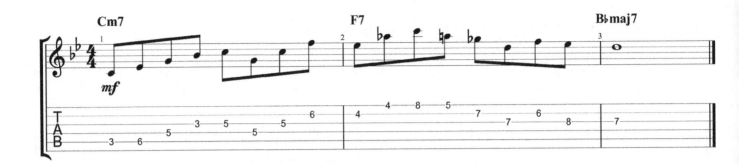

The second example demonstrates how "stacking" triads can yield some colourful, yet logical-sounding melodies with a fairly big range.

Over the Cm7 chord, the line is constructed by connecting Gm7 and Ebmaj7 arpeggios. The 5th and 7th of Gm7 are used to encircle the Eb.

The F7 line is constructed from Ab major and D major triads. The Ab major triad is in root position and the D major triad in first inversion. This creates the impression of an Ab7b9#11 arpeggio. Both triads have a repeated note added in order to fill the bar. The line resolves to the 9th (C) of Bbmaj7.

Example 5k

The diminished scale started to appear in jazz in the bebop era, but didn't become common until the hardbop phase. Quartal harmony also became popular around this time – based on stacked fourths rather than the stacked thirds that form the basis of Western harmony. In jazz, quartal harmony is used to bring a different colour to chords, rather than create a new way of viewing harmony.

Example 5l starts with a quartal arpeggio built from the 5th (G) of the Cm7 chord. From here the line continues with a C Minor Pentatonic scale melody. This time, the line played over the F7 chord combines B major and D major triads. The B major triad is not unique to the diminished sound since it is also diatonic to F# Melodic Minor (AKA the F Altered scale). The B major triad gives us the #11 (B), b7 (D#) and b9 (F#) intervals against an F root. Combined with the D major triad, we also have a 13th and a 3rd.

The construction of the melody is similar to Example 5j, where the 1st inversion B major triad connects to the D major triad in a voice-leading manner. The line resolves stepwise to the 5th (F) of Bbmaj7.

Example 5l

In Example 5m the line begins with an Eb major triad (built from the 3rd of Cm7), followed by a G Minor Pentatonic fragment. Over the F7 chord is a D major triad in first inversion and a root position Ab major triad. You may have noticed that I don't often use the F major triad because it doesn't add any colour and only so many 1/8th notes are available in a 4/4 bar!

In this example the melody relies on connecting the D and Ab major triads by linking the top two notes of the D triad to the lowest two notes of the Ab triad. (The last two notes of the bar could also be considered the top notes of a D major triad).

Example 5m

Example 5n uses a similar device – chaining triads together by using the last two notes of one triad to encircle the first note of the next.

The Cm7 line is a basic pattern Ebmaj7 arpeggio built from the 3rd of Cm7. The line is executed with legato technique to make is easier for the right hand to play the many string changes.

For the F7 chord, the line combines D, Ab and two notes of a B major triad. The D and Ab triads are in root position and the 5th of the D major is used to lead to the root of the Ab major triad. The last note of the Ab major triad could be seen as its 5th, but is also the 3rd of B major. The line ends with a 2nd inversion B major triad that resolves to the 5th (F) of Bbmaj7.

Example 5n

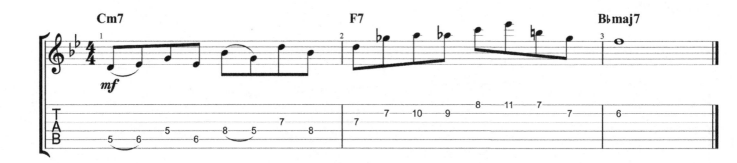

The problem with using the arpeggio built from the 5th of a minor chord is that it does not contain the 3rd, which is an important interval to communicate the sound of the chord. A standard way of dealing with this is to use the arpeggio to encircle the 3rd, demonstrated in Example 5o. From the 3rd, the line continues with a descending scale run to the 3rd (A) of F7.

The F7 line uses first inversion F major and B major triads. This combination highlights the #11 and b9 extensions. The line uses the #9 and b9 to resolve to the 7th (A) of Bbmaj7.

Example 5o

An interval skip of a 6th is a beautiful way to add variation to a scale run. The line played over the Cm7 in this example opens with an ascending 6th interval from G to Eb. The traditional counterpoint rule for a melody like this demands that the tension of the large ascending interval is resolved with step-wise motion in a descending direction. This musical "rule" doesn't always apply to jazz melodies, but the example below demonstrates how well it can work.

The line played over the F7 makes use of a root position F major and first inversion D major triad to spell out an F713b9 sound. The line is resolved via an Eb to the 3rd (D) of Bbmaj7.

Example 5p

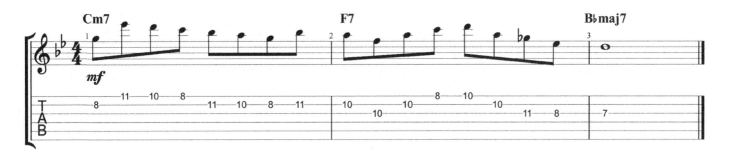

Embellishing an arpeggio by adding scale notes in between can be a good way to craft a melody that still has the chord tones on the beat but doesn't sound too predictable. The line on the Cm7 chord in this example is constructed in this manner using a Cm9 arpeggio. A D note is added in the lower octave between the C and Eb.

On the F7 chord, the line combines B and Ab major triads. Both are in first inversion and together they add a lot of colour with the b9, #9 and #11. The melody resolves to the 3rd (D) of Bbmaj7 via F and Eb.

Example 5q

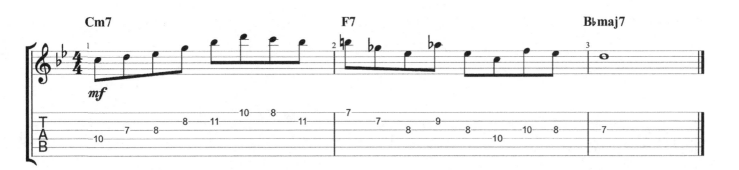

Inversions of arpeggios offer a lot of variation in terms of adding interval skips. In Example 5r the line over Cm7 has an Ebmaj7 arpeggio that begins on the root, but skips down to the G, then ascends the arpeggio. The remainder of the bar is a straight Cm7 arpeggio. This type of phrase is very common with George Benson and Grant Green. In fact, Grant Greens solo on I'll Remember April is almost entirely built on this phrase right from the pick-up.

In bar two, B major and A major triads are used over the F7 chord. The B major triad is in root position and the Ab major triad in second inversion. The connection between the two is the Eb note, which is the 3rd of B and the 5th of Ab. The line resolves via a B and Ab that work as a chromatic enclosure of the 7th (A) of Bbmaj7.

Example 5r

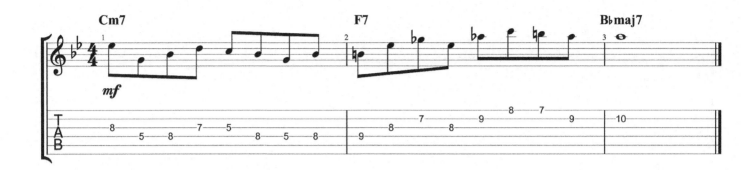

The quintal arpeggio is also a great open sounding structure to apply to a Cm7 chord. Here it is used from the Eb and spells out a Cm11 sound. The quintal arpeggio is preceded by a diatonic enclosure of the Eb.

Quintal Arpeggios (stacks of 5ths) are becoming very common melodic ideas in jazz. You will hear Jonathan Kreisberg and Kurt Rosenwinkel use them often in their solos and I will return to this topic later in this series.

The F7 line uses D and B major triads to create a line that quickly moves from the low Gb to the A positioned a 10th above. The D major triad is in first inversion and the B major triad in root position. The line concludes with an Ab that leads into the 7th (A) of Bbmaj7.

Example 5s

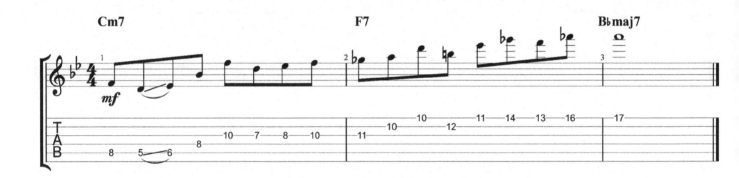

Chapter Assignments

Write a set of five or more licks over a progression, or a short solo, using:

Ab and D major triad pairs

Ab and B major triad pairs

Try experimenting with using open-voiced or "spread" versions of the triads

Stack triads to create a bigger structure, superimposing them over each other

Spend time practising free improvisation with the triads to understand them better and to help connect them on the fretboard. This exercise will prove useful for other scale sounds too.

Chapter Six – Put it in a Blues

This book has covered a wide range of ideas you can use to improvise over the II V I progression. To illustrate how to bring them all together in one piece of music, I composed a Bb blues solo. The aim of this piece is to show how the scale and arpeggio concepts can be applied in a realistic musical context.

By all means learn the full solo, but a great exercise is to break it down and pick out the phrases that appeal to you. After the transcription of the solo I have included a bar-by-bar analysis of how each line is constructed, but see if you can work out for yourself what's going on before turning to the answers! The solo is played like a solo (i.e. it's not exercises strung together), so in my explanation of the lines I focus on pointing out the concepts covered in this book. There is usually more than one way to think about a phrase played over a chord, so see if you come up with a different interpretation to me.

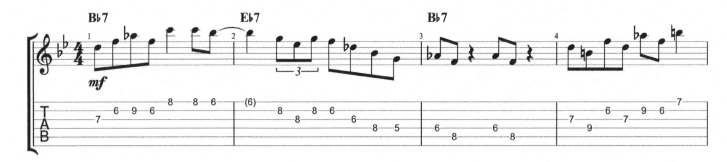

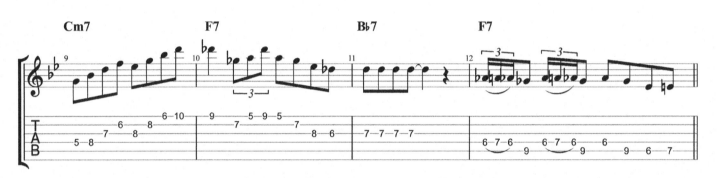

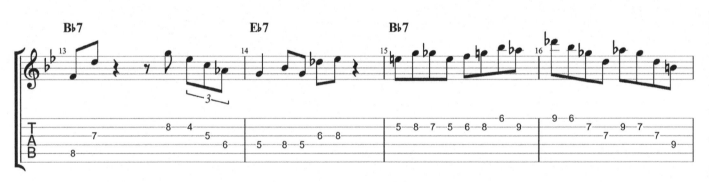

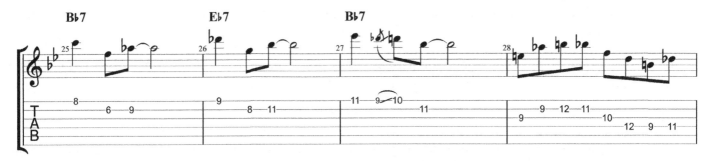

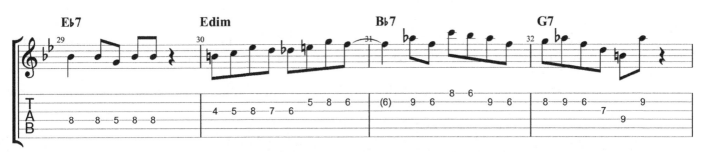

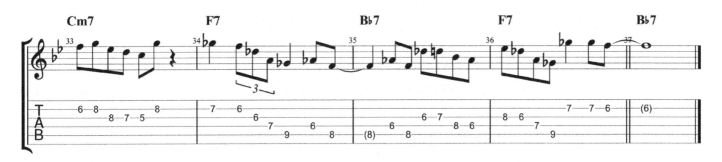

Solo Analysis

Chorus One

Bar 1 – The Bb7 line is based on the arpeggio from the 3rd = Dm7b5

Bar 2 – The Eb7 line consists firstly of an Eb major triad, then a descending Gm7b5 arpeggio (built from the 3rd of the chord).

Bar 4 – Uses the harmonic minor on Bb7 to pull towards the Eb7 (in this case playing the pattern of a Ddim arpeggio).

Bars 5-6 – This is a very common melodic trick which makes a statement over the Eb7 chord and repeats it over the Edim chord, altering it slightly to fit. The F note in bar 5 is changed to an E in bar 6.

Bar 8 – The G7 line is a fast minor II V using first a Dm7b5 arpeggio then a Bdim arpeggio.

Bar 9 – The Cm7 line is constructed by linking together arpeggios from its 5th and 3rd intervals (Gm7 and Ebmaj7).

Bar 10 – The F7 altered line can be analysed in two ways: an Ebm7b5 arpeggio over the whole bar, or a Gbm triad for the first half of the bar and an Ebm7b5 arpeggio inversion for the second half.

Bar one2 – The line over F7 uses the altered scale with two trills and a scale run with a chromatic passing note.

Chorus Two

Bar 13 – Uses an Abmaj7 diatonic arpeggio built from the 7th of Bb7.

Bar 14 – The melody consists of Eb7 arpeggio notes.

Bar 15 – A chromatic enclosure targets the F note on beat 3 and adds a passing Bb between G and Ab in the 2nd half of the bar.

Bar 16 – Suggests Bb7alt with Dmaj7#5 and 1st inversion Abm7b5 cascading arpeggios.

Bars 17-18 – a minor 3rd interval melody moves through the scale and repeats on the Edim chord.

Bar one9 – This line is an arpeggio from the 3rd of Bb7 with a chromatic passing note added to the descending scale run in the second half of the bar.

Bar 20 – There is a G7alt line built around an Fm7b5 arpeggio in the second half of the bar.

Bar 22 – The F7 line uses the diminished scale. D major and Ab major triads create an F7(13b9#9) sound.

Bar 24 – The F7 altered sound comes from linking together Amaj7#5 and Gbm triads.

Chorus Three

Bars 25-27 – Fm and Gdim triads are used to create a motif over Bb7 and Eb7 chords respectively. The motif concludes with a simple Bb statement in bar 27 that resolves back to the root.

Bar 28 – The line over Bb7 line uses E and Bb diminished scale triads.

Bar 30 – The line uses a chromatic enclosure to target the Db on beat 3, which is the first note of a Dbdim triad.

Bar 32 – C Harmonic Minor is used for the G7 chord. The melody uses a Bdim arpeggio.

Bar 33 – The melody from the previous bar is developed and repeated over the Cm7 with basic scale tones.

Bar 34 – This is an F7alt line using a Gbm(maj7) arpeggio.

Bar 35 – This is a Bb7 blues line constructed from the Bb7 arpeggio with a leading note before the 3rd.

Bar 36 – Here is an F7 altered line using a first inversion Ebm7b5 arpeggio that skips up to resolve to the 5th (F) of Bb7 which ends the solo.

Conclusion

Throughout this book we've looked at some of the essential building blocks of contemporary jazz guitar, personified by players such as Kurt Rosenwinkel, Jonathan Kreisberg, Gilad Hekselman, Adam Rogers and more. Building on the heritage of the jazz guitar legends, these modern players are taking the language of jazz guitar to new places. I hope I have imparted some useful tools and insights to assist you in creating that sound for yourself.

More than that, I hope I have inspired a desire to play more, experiment, and make these ideas your own. Nothing is set in stone. Feel free to adapt, change and fuse together my ideas until they express your musical preferences and become a natural part of *your* musical vocabulary. That is the point at which the ideas stop being mere concepts and become real music!

Have fun and keep practising,

Jens

More Jazz Books from Fundamental Changes

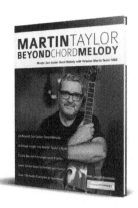

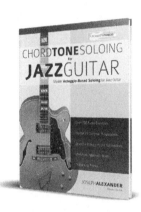
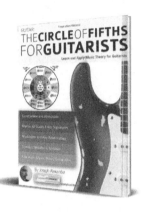
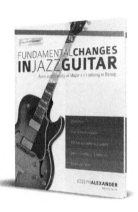

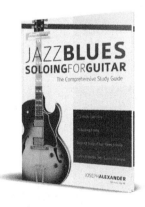
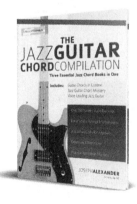

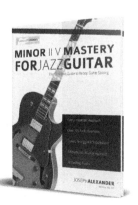